HTML5, CSS3, Javascript, JQuery Mobile Programming Beginning to End Cross-Platform App Design

STEPHEN LINK

ISBN: 1511583436
ISBN-13: 978-1511583435

DEDICATION

I would like to give thanks to my God. Without Him, life would be unbearable. Thanks also to my wife who has supported me through the research and study time required to complete this book.

Many thanks go out to the teachers and mentors who have inspired the creative thought process and provided ideas for program material. Without others, this is a cold, cruel world.

CONTENTS

ACKNOWLEDGMENTS

I would like to give thanks to my God. Without Him, life would be unbearable. Thanks also to my wife who has supported me through the research and study time required to complete this book

1 EXPLANATION OF CURRENT TECHNOLOGIES

HTML5, in its simplest form, is another version of the HTML specification. Previous versions would include 4.1, 3.2, and earlier. HTML stands for HyperText Markup Language. Why is version 5 so important? Because of the advances it has made in dynamic application design. Years ago web pages would tend to be static and quite boring, although they accomplished the purpose of displaying desired information. Today's web pages and apps can be designed with as much functionality as we have come to expect from stand-alone desktop applications. Incorporating video, navigation, and many other user-friendly functions on any device has become a quite normal expectation. Using HTML5 in combination with the other technologies explained in this EBook, you will acquire the ability to impress your users with the functionality that they need for everyday business functions.

CSS3 is another relatively new technology although Cascading Style Sheets have been around since 1996. As you may have guessed, CSS helps in styling and presenting your user interface. You can utilize CSS formatting within your individual HTML tags, known as in-line. You can also include a section of CSS code within the HEAD tag of your HTML page. This is known as an internal style sheet. A third way to implement cascading style sheets, and probably the most popular, is to use an external style sheet. All three methods can accomplish the same results and each has its own useful situations.

Let's say that you have a small site with only a few pages. In this case inline styling may work well. If you find that you have to apply the same styling to multiple elements, it would definitely be beneficial to use an internal style sheet. You would be able to define the style once and apply it as many times as necessary with minimal effort. Now let's carry this effort across multiple web pages and maybe even hundreds. You could define the styles in one external style sheet and include a link to it in every page. The simplicity provided by the external CSS approach is the reason for its popularity.

Javascript is a client-side language that has been around since the mid-2000s although the initial concept was known as "server side scripting" and was introduced in 1994. Now you have seen two terms which may seem contradictory - "client side" versus "server side." You probably guessed that the server, or web server, is the computer that generates the web pages that get sent to the user's computer. Good guess. The user's computer is the client; so this means that client-side processes run on the user's computer and report the results back to the server for additional processing. Any Javascript code that you write for today's systems runs as an interpreted client-side function. Oops, we threw another term out there - interpreted. The advantage of this execution methodology is that a single Javascript program can be run on many different platforms. It is loaded onto the client system and executed whether it is a Mac, PC, Linux, Android, or any number of other operating systems.

JQuery and **JQuery Mobile** (JQM) are packages that can be included into your web page or app so that you do not have to recreate the massive functionality provided by these plugins. Imagine having to chop down your own trees and mill your own lumber in order to be able to build a clubhouse. JQuery, JQM, and many other available plugins give you the ability to skip the low end function design and jump right into creativity mode. What kind of functionality? JQM is used mainly for user interface design while JQuery will allow much easier access to the components on screen. We will use both of these as the app is designed.

You may be wondering which editor you should use. Notepad will work fine if you are a hardcore HTML coder. Notepad++ works a little better than Notepad. Netbeans is my editor of choice for HTML and Java coding. Now let's hop right into the code design and explanation.

2 THE HEAD SECTION

The code in this section will help you to get started on the app. Since we are designing for HTML5 we use the "html" doctype. The next line of code sets up the appcache. What is the appcache used for? To speed up loading and execution of your mobile app. This will allow you to use a config file to control which files are loaded on the local device. You should be quite familiar with the next few lines with the opening head tag, title, and charset metatag.

This next line requires a little explanation since it is essential to auto sizing on various devices. It uses another metatag, viewport, which sets the width to device width (phone, tablet, desktop, etc) and it is scalable with an initial scale of 1. You could change these settings but they will work well as shown here for most applications. How does this one work? Let's say that you are on an android phone and use a "pinch" to expand the screen size. This will change the scaling used for your view.

Now we get to look at the plugins mentioned above. This app uses jQuery, jQuery mobile, and a google maps add in. These are incorporated using the script tag. We have previously mentioned JQuery and JQM, but what are we doing with Google? You will be quite impressed with the functionality shown in later sections using the geolocation functionality of the device.

```html
<!DOCTYPE html>
<html manifest="http://www.yourwebsite.com/quiz/quiz.appcache">
<head>
<title>Your Quiz Program</title>
<meta charset="UTF-8">
<meta name="viewport" content="width=device-width, initial-scale=1.0, user-scalable=yes">
<link rel="stylesheet" href="http://code.jquery.com/mobile/1.3.2/jquery.mobile-1.3.2.min.css" />
<script src="http://code.jquery.com/jquery-1.9.1.min.js"></script>
<script src="http://code.jquery.com/mobile/1.3.2/jquery.mobile-1.3.2.min.js"></script>
<script src="https://maps.googleapis.com/maps/api/js?v=3.exp&sensor=true"></script>
```

CSS3

Now we get to work with the CSS3 styles. Notice that we are still in the head tag and we are now using the style tag to incorporate this formatting functionality.

```
<style>
@font-face
{
font-family: headfont;
src: url(CamouflageW.ttf);
}
@media all
{
#seldiv
{
font-family: headfont;
font-size: 7vmin;
color: olive;
text-align: center
}
#findiv
{
font-family: headfont;
font-size: 4vmin;
color: olive;
text-align: center
}
#optimized
{
font-family: sans-serif;
font-size: 5vmin;
color: black;
text-align: left
}
#buttons,#qnbr,#qnbr2,#corrhdr,#finhdr
{
font-family: sans-serif;
height: 6vmin;
font-size: 5vmin;
}
#divabout,#quiz,#type,#quest1,#quest2,#txtq,#picq
{
font-family:sans-serif;
color:black;
font-size: 4vmin;
text-align: left
}
#map_canvas
{
width: 49%;
height: 65vmin;
float: left;
```

```
border: .2vmin solid black;
}
#directions-panel
{
height: 65vmin;
float: right;
width: 49%;
overflow: auto;
font-size: 2vmin !important;
}
#sign-img
{
width: 65%;
}
#fin-img
{
width: 90%;
}
}
}
body
{
background-color: lightgray
}
</style>
```

Did you type all of that? While you were typing did you wonder what each statement means? We will go through each of the commands and explain their functionality. See the appendix to download the zip file with all of the code included.

The first section sets the font to "CamouflageW" for the headfont family. What purpose does this have? Well, the initial target for this program was an environmental learning center and the camouflage style font looks quite nice for the intro page of the app. It was a nice added bonus that "CamouflageW" is available as a public domain font. What is the purpose of the "@media all" statement? That says that the CSS formatting shown between the brackets following it belong to all media. This "all" specification would include screen and print devices.

You may be wondering what all of these things refer to with the "#" in front of them. Each of these refers to a named div tag in your page. All formatting between the brackets following the tag apply to the specific section of the page. You will notice in the "seldiv" and "findiv" we assign the headfont using the font-family property. We also assign the font-size, color, and text-align properties. The names of these properties are rather self-explanatory although one item that you see requires explanation. When we set the font-size the "vmin" unit is used. This is a new unit available in CSS3 and it assists greatly in responsive design. Since the vmin unit depends on the browser viewport, let's look at an example. For a browser sized at 1,000x1,200 pixels, 1.5vmin will equal a 15px font size

In the next div assignments we see the ability to assign the properties for multiple divs by simply separating the names with a comma. We also see resetting of the font family to sans-serif and setting the height to a specific vmin setting. Looking down at the map_canvas div we see the use ofwidth as a percentage, float, and border. The border, as it implies, is a box drawn around the specific div. The float property assigns the attribute of being anchored to the left of the viewport.

In the directions-panel we see that it is floating right while the map_canvas floats left and both have a width of 49%. This works well to display both side by side without overlaying either of the div sections. The meaning of the "overflow: auto" property is that a scrollbar will appear if the content is too large to fit in the area. One more feature to note is the addition of "!important" rule to the font-size property. This forces the property to be applied regardless of any other formatting in place. Finally, we see CSS applied to the "body" section. Background-color is set to light-gray for the entire page body.

BEGINNING FUNCTIONALITY

We have seen the use of internal cascading style sheets to apply formatting to various portions of the page. Now we get into the main functionality of our app. This is also contained within a script tag with a type of "text/javascript."

```
<script type="text/javascript">
var cdarray = new Array();
var qarray = new Array();
var midarr = new Array();
var shortarr = new Array();
var qctr = 0;
var corrctr = 0;
var currq = 0;
var qtyp;
var ptyp;
var qdiff;
var q1;
var a1;
var a2;
var a3;
var a4;
var pic1;
var ans1;
var img;
var picnbr = 0;
var soundnbr = 0;
var snd;
var you = {};
var map = {};
var directionsService = new google.maps.DirectionsService();
var directionsDisplay;
```

Let's first take a look at a requirement of javascript programming - variable assignment. Although you could assign variables of a specific type such as string or numeric (single/double), we assign all variables as the "var" type. The meaning of this assignment method is that it will accept the type of whatever is assigned to it. If you assign a string surrounded by quotes it is taken as text. Assigning a number turns the variable into a numeric type.

3 FUNCTIONS

LOAD FUNCTION

Now for the individual functions of our app. A function, as shown below, is named using the "function" keyword. Following that is the function name and you can pass parameters into the function by placing them within the parentheses. Our first function is named "load" and it loads the quiz data from an XML file. You will notice words that come after "//." These are comments to make the meaning of the code clearer. You will also notice that each line ends with a semicolon (;). This is a requirement which indicates end of line to javascript.

```
function load()
{
ans1 = "";
ans12 = "";
var chk = jQuery('#quiz input:radio:checked');
qtyp = chk.attr('value');
chk = jQuery('#type input:radio:checked');
qdiff = chk.attr('value');
if (window.XMLHttpRequest)
{// code for IE7+, Firefox, Chrome, Opera, Safari
xmlhttp = new XMLHttpRequest();
}
else
{// code for IE6, IE5
xmlhttp = new ActiveXObject("Microsoft.XMLHTTP");
}
xmlhttp.open("GET", "questions.xml", false);
xmlhttp.send();
xmlDoc = xmlhttp.responseXML;
var x = xmlDoc.getElementsByTagName("QUESTION");
for (i = 0; i < x.length; i++)
{
cdarray[i] = new Array();
cdarray[i][0] =
x[i].getElementsByTagName("TYPE")[0].childNodes[0].nodeValue;
  cdarray[i][1] =
x[i].getElementsByTagName("DIFFICULTY")[0].childNodes[0].nodeValue;
  cdarray[i][2] =
x[i].getElementsByTagName("TEXT")[0].childNodes[0].nodeValue;
```

```
  cdarray[i][3] =
x[i].getElementsByTagName("ANSWER1")[0].childNodes[0].nodeValue;
  cdarray[i][4] =
x[i].getElementsByTagName("ANSWER2")[0].childNodes[0].nodeValue;
  if (x[i].getElementsByTagName("ANSWER3")[0].childNodes.length > 0)
  {
  cdarray[i][5] =
x[i].getElementsByTagName("ANSWER3")[0].childNodes[0].nodeValue;
  }
  else
  {
  cdarray[i][5] = "";
  }
  if (x[i].getElementsByTagName("ANSWER4")[0].childNodes.length > 0)
  {
  cdarray[i][6] =
x[i].getElementsByTagName("ANSWER4")[0].childNodes[0].nodeValue;
  }
  else
  {
  cdarray[i][6] = "";
  }
  cdarray[i][7] =
x[i].getElementsByTagName("CORRECT")[0].childNodes[0].nodeValue;
  if (x[i].getElementsByTagName("PICTURE")[0].childNodes.length > 0)
  {
  cdarray[i][8] =
x[i].getElementsByTagName("PICTURE")[0].childNodes[0].nodeValue;
  }
  if (cdarray[i][0] === qtyp && cdarray[i][1] === qdiff)
  {
  midarr[qctr] = new Array();
  midarr[qctr][0] = cdarray[i][0];
  midarr[qctr][1] = cdarray[i][1];
  midarr[qctr][2] = cdarray[i][2];
  midarr[qctr][3] = cdarray[i][3];
  midarr[qctr][4] = cdarray[i][4];
  midarr[qctr][5] = cdarray[i][5];
  midarr[qctr][6] = cdarray[i][6];
  midarr[qctr][7] = cdarray[i][7];
  arraylen = numProps(cdarray[i]);
  if (arraylen > 8)
  {
  midarr[qctr][8] = cdarray[i][8];
  }
  qctr++;
  }
  }
  shortarr = midarr.sort(randomSort2);
  for (i = 0; i < 10; i++)
  {
  qarray[i] = new Array();
  qarray[i][0] = midarr[i][0];
```

```
qarray[i][1] = midarr[i][1];
qarray[i][2] = midarr[i][2];
qarray[i][3] = midarr[i][3];
qarray[i][4] = midarr[i][4];
qarray[i][5] = midarr[i][5];
qarray[i][6] = midarr[i][6];
qarray[i][7] = midarr[i][7];
arraylen = numProps(midarr[i]);
if (arraylen > 8)
{
qarray[i][8] = midarr[i][8];
}
}
currq = 0;
arraylen = numProps(qarray[0]);
if (arraylen > 8)
{
q1 = qarray[currq][2];
a1 = qarray[currq][3];
a2 = qarray[currq][4];
a3 = qarray[currq][5];
a4 = qarray[currq][6];
ans1 = qarray[currq][7];
pic1 = qarray[currq][8];
document.getElementById("q-img").src = pic1;
}
else
{
q1 = qarray[currq][2];
a1 = qarray[currq][3];
a2 = qarray[currq][4];
a3 = qarray[currq][5];
a4 = qarray[currq][6];
ans1 = qarray[currq][7];
}
nextquestion();
}
```

Well, that was a lot of typing! Now we get to find out what all of that code is doing. First, let's look at a couple of structures that you see repeated many times. These would be the "IF-ELSE" statements and the "FOR" statements. An "IF" statement will compare two items and perform the functionality that is between the brackets following it. If there is an "ELSE" statement after the brackets (and the statement is false) it will fall through and execute the statements in the brackets below it. A "FOR" statement is known as a loop and it executes statements a specified number of times. As with the "IF" statement, it executes all statements in the brackets following it until the last execution has been performed.

You will see that we are using some of the variables declared at the top of our script and they are either being set to empty or the contents of items on the page. Our third line assigns a new variable that was not previously assigned using the "var" command. It also sets the contents of that variable to the checked item of the "quiz" div. As you can see by the terms used, this is a radio input and the variable is being set to the selected item. Next we set the qtyp variable to the value of the selected radio item. We repeat this approach to set the qdiff variable. These represent the type of questions selected and the difficulty.

The next "IF-ELSE" section of code determines how we are going to open the XML file depending on the browser version. The specific versions are illustrated in the comment code. The "xmlhttp.open" command actually sets up the command to open while the following "send" opens the XML file for reading. Next we read the entire XML file into the xmlDoc variable and separate individual groups by the tagname "QUESTION." The number of questions in the file is assigned to the variable "x" and we go into a "FOR" loop to cycle through each of the individual questions.

By assigning cdarray[i] to a new array we are creating a new group of questions with each pass through this loop while "i" indicates the number of iterations through. As we go through the loop, we are assigning question type, difficulty, text, answer1, and answer2 for every question. You will notice an "IF" statement for answers 3 and 4. This is required to determine that they are not empty before assigning the variable. If they are empty (NULL) an error will be thrown if an attempt is made to assign that to a variable. Every question will have a correct answer so we do not have to verify that it is populated but every question will not have a picture so we have to check for that also. You have seen the use of "getelementsbytagname" to read data from the XML file and that is coupled with the index[0], childnodes[0], and nodevalue to retrieve the individual field.

In the next "IF" statement we are determining if the question just loaded fits the selected type and difficulty. If so, it is being assigned to an array named "midarr" using the same approach you have just seen. Something new to this logic is the use of "numProps." This is actually a user defined function which determines the number of properties in an array. It serves the same function as the "check for empty" that we did above but it is much more efficient and works since the array properties have already been assigned. The "numProps" function will be explained in a later section. The last line you see before the next iteration of our FOR loop increments "qctr" so that we can keep track of how many selected questions have been accumulated.

Our next command randomly sorts our selected questions. The following loop selects the first ten questions in that sorted list and assigns them to "qarray." This means that even if there are only ten questions within a type and difficulty they will not always appear in the same order. Once again we use the "numProps" function to determine the length of the array and assign picture only if it exists.

The final section of this code sets the current question to the first (0) and determines the number of properties to decide whether to display the picture. If there is a picture it uses "document.getelementbyid to set the src for "q-img" to the corresponding picture file. This will actually set the source for the image element. The function that we are processing next is nextquestion().

NUMPROPS FUNCTION

We had mentioned "numProps" previously. That is the next function that we will cover. If you remember, we can pass parameters inside of the parentheses. In this case we are passing in an object. Although the object could be basically any type of element, we are passing in an array and this function is using the "hasownproperty" method to count the number of keys contained in the array. That is how we determine if the array has a length of seven or eight (with or without picture). Another new feature shown in this function is a return variable. After counting the elements and determining the length, that length is passed back to the calling routine. In the case of the previous section of code, this is assigned to the "arraylen" variable.

```
function numProps(obj)
{
var c = 0;
for (var key in obj)
{
if (obj.hasOwnProperty(key))
```

```
++c;
}
return c;
}
```

ISCORRECT FUNCTION

The next function that we will review is titled "iscorrect." The purpose of this function is to determine if the selected answer is the correct answer. You have already seen this approach of reading the value from the selected item. This is actually designed to handle questions with (ans1) or without (ans12) pictures. Something that may need a little explanation in this function is the use of OR (||) between the items in the "IF" statement. This checks for either of these to be correct and redirects processing to the corranswer() function if that is the case and incorranswer() if not.

```
function iscorrect()
{
var chk = jQuery('#txtq input:radio:checked');
qtyp = chk.attr('value');
chk = jQuery('#picq input:radio:checked');
ptyp = chk.attr('value');
if (qtyp === ans1 || ptyp === ans12)
{
corranswer();
}
else
{
incorranswer();
}
}
```

ANSWER FUNCTIONS

Because of the similarity in design, we will cover both incorranswer() and corranswer() in this section. First, review the code for both.

```
function incorranswer()
{
document.getElementById("corrhdr").innerHTML = "Try again";
picnbr = Math.floor((Math.random() * 5) + 1);
soundnbr = Math.floor((Math.random() * 5) + 1);
switch (picnbr)
{
case 1:
document.getElementById("img").src = "rockin_no.gif";
break;
case 2:
```

```
document.getElementById("img").src = "ypmarsanim_no.gif";
break;
case 3:
document.getElementById("img").src = "scared_mouse_no.gif";
break;
case 4:
document.getElementById("img").src = "cgpinkellie_no.gif";
break;
case 5:
document.getElementById("img").src = "coolcow_no.gif";
break;
}
switch (soundnbr)
{
case 1:
document.getElementById("play").src = "boing_no.mp3";
document.getElementById("play").type = "audio/mpeg";
break;
case 2:
document.getElementById("play").src = "wahwah_no.mp3";
document.getElementById("play").type = "audio/mpeg";
break;
case 3:
document.getElementById("play").src = "Laugh_no.mp3";
document.getElementById("play").type = "audio/mpeg";
break;
case 4:
document.getElementById("play").src = "buzzer2_no.mp3";
document.getElementById("play").type = "audio/mpeg";
break;
case 5:
document.getElementById("play").src = "Buzzer_no.mp3";
document.getElementById("play").type = "audio/mpeg";
break;
}
if (ans12 !== "")
{
jQuery('#12').attr('checked', false);
jQuery('#12').checkboxradio('refresh');
jQuery('#22').attr('checked', false);
jQuery('#22').checkboxradio('refresh');
jQuery('#32').attr('checked', false);
jQuery('#32').checkboxradio('refresh');
jQuery('#42').attr('checked', false);
jQuery('#42').checkboxradio('refresh');
}
else
{
jQuery('#1').attr('checked', false);
jQuery('#1').checkboxradio('refresh');
jQuery('#2').attr('checked', false);
jQuery('#2').checkboxradio('refresh');
jQuery('#3').attr('checked', false);
```

```
jQuery('#3').checkboxradio('refresh');
jQuery('#4').attr('checked', false);
jQuery('#4').checkboxradio('refresh');
}
currq++;
ans12 = "";
ans1 = "";
jQuery.mobile.changePage(jQuery("#corr"));
}
function corranswer()
{
document.getElementById("corrhdr").innerHTML = "Correct";
picnbr = Math.floor((Math.random() * 5) + 1);
soundnbr = Math.floor((Math.random() * 5) + 1);
switch (picnbr)
{
case 1:
document.getElementById("img").src = "turtle_yes.gif";
break;
case 2:
document.getElementById("img").src = "fiddlin_coon_yes.gif";
break;
case 3:
document.getElementById("img").src = "dancing_elephant_yes.gif";
break;
case 4:
document.getElementById("img").src = "mag01_yes.gif";
break;
case 5:
document.getElementById("img").src = "lafrogkiss_yes.gif";
break;
}
switch (soundnbr)
{
case 1:
document.getElementById("play").src = "coocoo_yes.mp3";
document.getElementById("play").type = "audio/mpeg";
break;
case 2:
document.getElementById("play").src = "slide_yes.mp3";
document.getElementById("play").type = "audio/mpeg";
break;
case 3:
document.getElementById("play").src = "cheer_yes.mp3";
document.getElementById("play").type = "audio/mpeg";
break;
case 4:
document.getElementById("play").src = "crowd_yes.mp3";
document.getElementById("play").type = "audio/mpeg";
break;
case 5:
document.getElementById("play").src = "clapping_yes.mp3";
document.getElementById("play").type = "audio/mpeg";
```

```
break;
}
if (ans12 !== "")
{
jQuery('#12').attr('checked', false);
jQuery('#12').checkboxradio('refresh');
jQuery('#22').attr('checked', false);
jQuery('#22').checkboxradio('refresh');
jQuery('#32').attr('checked', false);
jQuery('#32').checkboxradio('refresh');
jQuery('#42').attr('checked', false);
jQuery('#42').checkboxradio('refresh');
}
else
{
jQuery('#1').attr('checked', false);
jQuery('#1').checkboxradio('refresh');
jQuery('#2').attr('checked', false);
jQuery('#2').checkboxradio('refresh');
jQuery('#3').attr('checked', false);
jQuery('#3').checkboxradio('refresh');
jQuery('#4').attr('checked', false);
jQuery('#4').checkboxradio('refresh');
}
currq++;
corrctr++;
ans1 = "";
ans12 = "";
jQuery.mobile.changePage(jQuery("#corr"));
}
```

In the first line of these functions we set the innerhtml element to display the phrase "Try Again" or "Correct." Next we choose a random picture to display and sound to play. Notice that we display only five of each although there can be many different selections.

Let's say that we want to use 25 different pictures. You would change picnbr to use 25 instead of 5 and would have 25 "case" statements for the picnbr "SWITCH" block. We just mentioned a new term - switch. That command has the same purpose as many consecutive "IF" statements but it works much more efficiently. The reason that it is more efficient is that it determines the value of the variable in parentheses (picnbr) and goes directly to the block of code corresponding to that number. From a logical standpoint, it is as if you do not have 5 (or 50 or 500, for that matter). Processing goes directly to the "CASE" block for that specific number and executes all code until it hits a "BREAK" statement. After that statement it does not see anything after until the ending brace for the "SWITCH" statement.

Inside of the picnbr "case" blocks we are setting an image, which you have already seen. Inside of the soundnbr "case" blocks we are setting a mpg audio file to play. The reason for the two statements used here are for compatibility purposes. In some cases (iphone, ipad, some Android devices, probably others) the audio file will not start automatically. The second command tells the audio player displayed on screen which type of sound file is being played. Our final "IF" block resets the selected answer in preparation for the next question.

The following three (or four) lines of code increment the question number and the correct counter in addition to resetting the currently correct answer variable. The final line of this section of code shows a new JQM function - changepage. This will redirect the page display to a new page. We can't use the standard "redirect" or javascript "window.location" because we are using the functionality of JQuery Mobile to place the separate display pages within one HTML page.

CLEARRB FUNCTION

If you are a seasoned javascript programmer you may recognize some of the functions used in this program. It is possible that at least two are unmodified function downloads from web sources. That would be the numProp function and the next, clearRB. I want to give credit where it is due but you can find many similar functions repeated across various sources and it is hard to credit the original author.

```
function clearRB(buttonGroup)
{
for (i = 0; i < buttonGroup.length; i++)
{
buttonGroup[i].removeAttr('checked');// uncheck it
}
}
```

This function is accepting a buttongroup as the parameter. It will cycle through all of the buttons in the group and clear the checked status of them. The original code that was implemented would check to see if the item was checked. That part was removed because there are no more than four items in the buttongroup.

NEXTQUESTION FUNCTION

Next we will see the "nextquestion" function. You may recall that this is the function called at the end of our "load" function. You can review the lengthy function and then we will cover some of the new logic that it contains.

```
function nextquestion()
{
if (currq < 10)
{
arraylen = numProps(qarray[currq]);
if (arraylen > 8)
{
q2 = qarray[currq][2];
a12 = qarray[currq][3];
a22 = qarray[currq][4];
a32 = qarray[currq][5];
a42 = qarray[currq][6];
ans12 = qarray[currq][7];
pic12 = qarray[currq][8];
document.getElementById("qnbr2").innerHTML = "Question " + (currq +
1).toString();
document.getElementById("quest2").innerHTML = q2;
document.getElementById("ans12").innerHTML = a12;
document.getElementById("ans22").innerHTML = a22;
```

```
if (a32 !== "")
{
document.getElementById("ans32").innerHTML = a32;
document.getElementById("q32").style.display = "block";
}
else
{
document.getElementById("q32").style.display = "none";
}
if (a42 !== "")
{
document.getElementById("ans42").innerHTML = a42;
document.getElementById("q42").style.display = "block";
}
else
{
document.getElementById("q42").style.display = "none";
}
document.getElementById("q-img").src = pic12;
jQuery.mobile.changePage(jQuery("#questionpic"));
}
else
{
q1 = qarray[currq][2];
a1 = qarray[currq][3];
a2 = qarray[currq][4];
a3 = qarray[currq][5];
a4 = qarray[currq][6];
ans1 = qarray[currq][7];
document.getElementById("qnbr").innerHTML = "Question " + (currq +
1).toString();
document.getElementById("quest1").innerHTML = q1;
document.getElementById("ans1").innerHTML = a1;
document.getElementById("ans2").innerHTML = a2;
if (a3 !== "")
{
document.getElementById("ans3").innerHTML = a3;
document.getElementById("q3").style.display = "block";
}
else
{
document.getElementById("q3").style.display = "none";
}
if (a4 !== "")
{
document.getElementById("ans4").innerHTML = a4;
document.getElementById("q4").style.display = "block";
}
else
{
document.getElementById("q4").style.display = "none";
}
jQuery.mobile.changePage(jQuery("#questiontxt"));
```

```
}
}
else
{
finish();
}
}
```

The purpose of the first "IF" statement is to check if we have asked the last question. You may have noticed that everything seems to start at 0. That is because javascript is a zero-based language. When you count to 10 and start with 0 the last number is 9. Because of this we check that the question counter is less than 10 in order to continue with question display.

Next you see the use of the "numProps" function to determine if this question group has a picture. Following that we set variables to the individual items of "qarray" and display those values on our page using the "innerHTML" property of each element. Notice that we are using a question number label to show the current question number to the user. After that we populate the question and first two answers.

Next we add a new approach that may be unfamiliar - hiding the last two question variables if they are not needed. This is the reason for checking if "ans..." is not equal (!==) to nothing. If it has been populated we set the value and set the "style.display" to "block" which serves the purpose of making it visible.Otherwise we set "style.display" to "none" so that it is invisible. This hides the radio buttons in the cases where there are only two or three of them.

The last two statements of the "picture" block have the function of setting the picture to be displayed with the question and transferring to the "questionpic" page to display the values we have just set up.

The other side of the "IF" statement displays the question without picture and transfers to the "questiontxt" page. This is using the same functionality other than displaying the picture. The first "IF" statement checked to see if we had displayed the last question and transferred execution to the "finish" function if so. We will review that function next.

FINISH FUNCTION

The "finish" function is quite brief and simple. It sets the variable to display the correct number of answers and displays the "finish" page. Just as a reminder, this uses the "corrctr" that was incremented every time that a correct answer was given.

```
function finish()
{
document.getElementById("finhdr").innerHTML = "Correct answers " +
corrctr.toString();
jQuery.mobile.changePage(jQuery("#finish"));
}
```

GETLOC FUNCTION

Now we get into what I consider the really fun part of this app - using geolocation and Google Maps to display directions to a specific location. This is really useful if you have drawn someone in with the quiz questions and the information provided by them. Now they want to visit the sponsoring organization. Credit for this code goes to the Google Support group.

```
function getLoc()
{
  if (navigator.geolocation)
  {
  //if the browser supports geolocation, get current location and display on
a map.
  var gps = navigator.geolocation;
  directionsDisplay = new google.maps.DirectionsRenderer();
  gps.getCurrentPosition(function(position)
{
  var latLng = new google.maps.LatLng(position.coords.latitude,
position.coords.longitude);
  var opts = {zoom: 8, center: latLng, mapTypeId:
google.maps.MapTypeId.ROADMAP};
  map = new google.maps.Map($("map_canvas"), opts);
  you = new google.maps.Marker({position: latLng, map: map, title: "There you
are!"});
  var infowindow = new google.maps.InfoWindow(
{
  map: map,
  position: latLng,
  content: 'Your location'
  });
  directionsDisplay.setMap(map);
  directionsDisplay.setPanel(document.getElementById('directions-panel'));
  // Let's visit the White House
  var request =
{
  origin: latLng,
  destination: "1600 Pennsylvania Ave NW,20500",
  travelMode: google.maps.TravelMode.DRIVING
  };
  directionsService.route(request, function(response, status)
{
  if (status === google.maps.DirectionsStatus.OK)
{
  directionsDisplay.setDirections(response);
  }
  });
  });
  }
else
{
  //if the browser doesn't support geolocation, display an alert saying so.
  alert("Your browser doesn't support geolocation.");
  }
```

}

The truly interesting part about geolocation, aside from the newness of this capability, is the fact that three different methods can be used to determine your current location. Are you on a smartphone or tablet that has geolocation functionality enabled? If so, this will provide the most accurate location. If there is no localized geolocation functionality the next option is to pull the location of the cell tower that you are using. This will generally give a relatively close current location. Are you using a desktop which obviously does not have geolocation functionality but the browser in use supports that? Your current IP address will be used to determine a starting location.

Now that we have covered some of the semantics of the geolocation process, let's get into the logic of this routine. The first "IF" statement determines if you have geolocation capability. If not, you will get a message stating that. Next we set a variable named "gps" to the current location using the "navigator.geolocation" method. Next we set our directions display to a Google Maps DirectionsRenderer and feed the "position" function into the GetCurrentPosition method. The next few lines of code set up the options, create the map, and set/display the current position.

The next section of code incorporates the driving instructions with the currently determined location as the starting point. The div used to display the driving directions is "directions-panel" and now you set the previously determined origin, destination address, and set the travel mode as driving (you could also use bicycling, transit or walking). Next we get the route from Google Maps and display it.

You will notice that there is not a whole lot of detail about this function given here. The Google Maps API can provide much more functionality beyond the basic features used here. A web search (Google, perhaps) will provide a wealth of information on using the Google Maps API in your programming.

RANDOMSORT2 FUNCTION

Next you will see another function which is believed to be unmodified from the version downloaded through the web. This performs a random sort and was called from the "load" function shown earlier. Notice that the first variable, "temp," is using 10 as the random number. This is because we have set the number of questions to be displayed at 10. This routine then goes through a couple of odd/even and pos/neg determinations before returning a number based on these.

```
function randomSort2(a, b)
{
  // Get a random number between 0 and 10
  var temp = parseInt(Math.random() * 10);
  // Get 1 or 0, whether temp is odd or even
  var isOddOrEven = temp % 2;
  // Get +1 or -1, whether temp greater or smaller than 5
  var isPosOrNeg = temp > 5 ? 1 : -1;
  // Return -1, 0, or +1
  return(isOddOrEven * isPosOrNeg);
```

ID FUNCTION

Have you realized that you are still in the HEAD tag of the page? Yes, you are. We will finally cover the last function and move into the individual pages used in this app. Now we will get to see a function that is required by the Google Maps API that was used. You will also notice that there are various places in our code where "jquery.mobile" was used and you may have been tempted to use a "$." This function is the reason that shortcut will not work. Without this function you can use the "$" in place of "jquery.mobile" and the geolocation stops working. Since there is basically only one line of code in this Google API function, explanation is not considered necessary.

```
    function $(id)
{
    //gets an element by the id passed to it.
    return document.getElementById(id);
    }
</script>
    </head>
```

4 PAGES

INDEX PAGE

Now we can finally get into the body and see the display of the pages and elements that we have been setting up in our javascript code. First we will cover a few details of formatting JQuery Mobile (JQM) pages. JQM uses data roles to determine where to display a specific element. That is why you will see data roles of page, header, content, button, footer, etc. The label of these roles is quite self-explanatory but if you need additional detail it can be found with a search using your favorite engine. You will also notice an "ID" assigned to the role of page. This is what we use to display the specific page as it is called by a button or changepage javascript.

```
<body>
<div data-role="page" id="index">
<div data-role="header">
<h1>This is where you have a header</h1>
</div>
<div data-role="content" id="seldiv" style="font-family:headfont;
color:olive">Welcome to the<br>
<img alt="Test" id="sign-img" src="<your favorite image>"><br>
Quiz Show
<a href="#begin" data-role="button">Begin</a>
<a href="#about" data-role="button">About</a>
<div id="optimized">
Optimized for <a href="www.mozilla.org/en-US/firefox/"
target="_blank">Firefox</a> 25+ and <a href="http://www.google.com/chrome"
target="_blank">Chrome</a> 31+<br>Compatible with iOS and most mobile
browsers<br>
Design and programming by Steve Link, Link Em Up
</div>
</div>
<div data-role="footer" data-position="fixed">
copyright 2014
</div>
</div>
```

Here we have the index page of the site. This will be the first page shown and allow navigation using the buttons shown on the page. You will notice that we are using inline CSS formatting in the "content" of this page in addition to the internal style sheet approach illustrated earlier. Also notice the header and footer roles which are displayed in the expected positions of the page. The footer has a position of "fixed" so that it will always be displayed at the bottom of the viewport regardless of how large the actual page height happens to be. Something to note here is the use of the button role instead of standard HTML buttons. This works much better with JQM formatting and the buttons will span the entire width of the viewport (or grid if the buttons are placed inside of a grid utilizing other formatting). Also notice the target of the button which uses "#" in front of the actual page id.

ABOUT PAGE

Now we will look at the "About" page which also calls the geolocation routine that we saw earlier.

```
<div data-role="page" id="about">
<div data-role="header" >
<h1>About</h1>
<a data-role="button" data-rel="back" data-icon="back" data-
iconpos="notext"></a>
</div>
<div data-role="content" id="divabout">
Design and programming by Steve Link, Link Em Up<br>
Questions and other supporting data provided by
Advisors and others. Their web site can be viewed at <a
href="http://www.whitehouse.gov" target="_blank">White House web site</a><br>
<a data-role="button" onclick="getLoc();">Getting to White House</a>
<div id="directions-panel"></div>
<div id="map_canvas"></div>
</div>
<div data-role="footer" data-position="fixed">
Your footer goes here
</div>
</div>
```

Notice that in the header we have included a button with data-rel and data-icon of "back." This also has an iconpos of "notext." The purpose of this is to place a back arrow icon on the left side of the header with no text displayed. In the content we are using the White House as the sponsoring agency. It would be nice to get on that government contract although this was not the original sponsor of this program.

Now we get to the fun part of calling the geolocation routine and displaying the results. Before clicking the button labeled "Getting to ..." you will see two empty sections below it. After clicking, you may be prompted to allow access to the geolocation function and then these areas will be populated with a map showing your current location on the left and driving directions on the right. Remember that these divs have a 49% width so the distance between them will be relative to the viewport size.

We should also point out something interesting about the different geolocation approaches. This is being written on my desktop machine and the web site is accessed using IE10 and it works well on this version of IE. The geolocation feature, however, is quite inaccurate based on my IP. It looks like my current location is 62 miles southwest compared to my actual location. This is truly a nice feature for mobile devices, though. It should be noted that later execution was able to locate my exact location even though I am on a desktop system.

BEGIN PAGE

This is the page where the user selects the type and difficulty of the quiz questions.

```
<div data-role="page" id="begin">
<div data-role="header">
<h1>Question types?</h1>
</div>
<div id="divbegin">
<div id="quiz">
Select your quiz type:<br>
<input type="radio" name="QuizType" id="cat1" value="Forestry">
<label for="cat1">Forestry</label>
<input type="radio" name="QuizType" id="cat2" value="Wildlife">
<label for="cat2">Wildlife</label>
<input type="radio" name="QuizType" id="cat3" value="Environmental">
<label for="cat3">Environmental</label>
</div>
<div id="type">
and the level of questions<br>
<input type="radio" name="Difficulty" id="Tadpole" value="Tadpole">
<label for="Tadpole">Tadpole</label>
<input type="radio" name="Difficulty" id="Bullfrog" value="Bullfrog">
<label for="Bullfrog">Bullfrog</label>
</div>
<a data-role="button" onclick="load();">Continue</a>
</div>
<div data-role="footer" data-position="fixed">
Your footer goes here
</div>
</div>
```

On the front page you saw a button labeled "Begin" with a target of "#begin." This is the page that is loaded after clicking on that button. On this page we are using two radio button groups named "QuizType" and "Difficulty." The javascript previously displayed read the checked item from both of these button groups to determine the selected type and difficulty. We see another button which uses the onclick() event to call the "load" function when it is clicked.

QUESTION PAGES

We will now cover both the "questiontxt" and "questionpic" pages due to their similarity.

```
<div data-role="page" id="questiontxt">
<div data-role="header">
<div id="qnbr"></div>
</div>
<div id="txtq">
<h6>Answer the question and click Next</h6>
<div id="quest1">q1</div>
<div id="q1"><input type="radio" name="answers" id="1" value="1">
<label for="1"><span id="ans1">q1</span></label></div>
```

```
<div id="q2"><input type="radio" name="answers" id="2" value="2">
<label for="2"><span id="ans2">q1</span></label></div>
<div id="q3"><input type="radio" name="answers" id="3" value="3">
<label for="3"><span id="ans3">q1</span></label></div>
<div id="q4"><input type="radio" name="answers" id="4" value="4">
<label for="4"><span id="ans4">q1</span></label></div>
<input data-role="button" id="txtcont" type="submit" value="Next"
onclick="iscorrect()">
</div>
<div data-role="footer" data-position="fixed">
Your footer goes here
</div>
</div>
<div data-role="page" id="questionpic">
<div data-role="header">
<div id="qnbr2"></div>
</div>
<div id="picq">
<h6>Answer the question and click Next</h6>
<div id="quest2">q1</div>
<img alt="image" id="q-img" src="">
<div id="q12"><input type="radio" name="answers2" id="12" value="1">
<label for="12"><span id="ans12">q1</span></label></div>
<div id="q22"><input type="radio" name="answers2" id="22" value="2">
<label for="22"><span id="ans22">q1</span></label></div>
<div id="q32"><input type="radio" name="answers2" id="32" value="3">
<label for="32"><span id="ans32">q1</span></label></div>
<div id="q42"><input type="radio" name="answers2" id="42" value="4">
<label for="42"><span id="ans42">q1</span></label></div>
<input data-role="button" id="piccont" type="submit" value="Next"
onclick="iscorrect()">
</div>
<div data-role="footer" data-position="fixed">
Your footer goes here
</div>
</div>
```

Hmmm … You may be wondering why these pages are leading off with an empty "qnbr" and "qnbr2" header. That has a quite simple answer. These pages are loaded from javascript code which is populating that div with the current question number. For proof, take a look above at the "nextquestion" function. Next we are using a radio group with the individual items populated using that same function. Finally, the button displayed uses the onclick event to call the "iscorrect" function which determines whether the user has selected the correct answer.

CORRECT PAGE

This page, with an id of "correct," is actually used even when the answer is incorrect.

```
<div data-role="page" id="corr">
<div data-role="header">
<div id="corrhdr"></div>
```

```
</div>
<div id="pic"><img alt="Test" id="img" src=""></div>
<div id="snd"><audio id="play" controls autoplay></audio></div>
<input data-role="button" id="nxtquest" type="submit" value="Next"
onclick="nextquestion()">
<div data-role="footer" data-position="fixed">
Your footer goes here
</div>
</div>
```

Once again, we have a div labeled "corrhdr" which is populated using either the "corranswer" or "incorranswer" function. We also have an image and audio player which is being assigned by those functions. The button on this screen uses the onclick event to call the "nextquestion" function.

FINISH PAGE

The final page in our app, of course, is the "finish" page. As we have previously seen, finhdr is assigned by the "finish" function. We are once again using inline CSS font formatting in addition to the internal CSS assignment used in the "head" section of our page.

```
<div data-role="page" id="finish">
<div data-role="header">
<div id="finhdr"></div>
</div>
<div data-role="content" id="findiv" style="font-family:headfont;
color:olive">
<img alt="Test" id="fin-img" src="your favorite image"><br>
When one tugs at a single thing in nature, he finds it attached to the rest
of the world. - John Muir
</div>
<div data-role="footer" data-position="fixed">
Your footer goes here
</div>
</div>
</body>
</html>
```

21 CREATING THE XML FILE

You have completed the web-based app and anyone can load the page if you have a web host to make it available to the world or host it on your own computer using an outside IP redirection service. Any users can even click on the "About" button and utilize the geolocation feature implemented into your site. That is impressive but it is not the main function of this app.

This section will show you how to create the XML file which is the main data source behind this program. If you have an extremely persistent and patient personality, you could use a standard text editor to fill in the following structure and save it as "questions.xml." See the "load" function if you want to change the name of this file. This uses a rather simple XML structure, shown below.

```xml
<?xml version="1.0" encoding="utf-8"?>
<QUIZ>
<QUESTION>
<TYPE>Cat1</TYPE>
<DIFFICULTY>Level1</DIFFICULTY>
<TEXT>_____ is the scientific study of plants</TEXT>
<ANSWER1>Botany</ANSWER1>
<ANSWER2>Geography</ANSWER2>
<ANSWER3>Rocket science</ANSWER3>
<ANSWER4>Astrology</ANSWER4>
<CORRECT>1</CORRECT>
<PICTURE></PICTURE>
</QUESTION>
<QUESTION>
<TYPE>Cat1</TYPE>
<DIFFICULTY>Level1</DIFFICULTY>
<TEXT>The following is a leaf form which type of tree?</TEXT>
<ANSWER1>Maple</ANSWER1>
<ANSWER2>Pine</ANSWER2>
<ANSWER3>Cherry</ANSWER3>
<ANSWER4>Cotton wood</ANSWER4>
<CORRECT>1</CORRECT>
<PICTURE>MapleLeaf.jpg</PICTURE>
</QUESTION>
</QUIZ>
```

In this file you will place a type equivalent to whatever your program used. In the case of this sample program type would be Forestry, Wildlife, or Environmental while Difficulty would be assigned either Tadpole or Bullfrog. Do you like the nature reference used there?

In the TEXT tag you will place the question while a minimum of two answers are required. If ANSWER3 or ANSWER4 will not be used you should still place the tags there with nothing in between (i.e. "<ANSWER3></ANSWER3>"). The CORRECT tag contains the correct answer number. Picture is also not required and this sample displays a first question with no picture while the second question illustrates how to duplicate multiple questions and utilize the picture.

As stated, the approach of editing this file in a text editor will work fine for someone who is patient and persistent. If you want to make this program available to a local science museum, for example, you will probably need a familiar user interface for question entry and maintenance. My chosen approach, due to a familiarity with VBA and Excel, is Microsoft Excel coupled with a macro to create the XML file. As with some of the previously utilized functions, the VBA code used in this Excel file was downloaded from an internet source and heavily modified to fit this function. We will display the VBA code here and you will receive the entire file in the source code download shown in the Appendix.

```vba
Sub CreateXML()
Dim HeaderR As Range
Dim R As Long
Dim C As Long
Dim FNum As Integer
Dim FName As Variant
Dim RR As Range
Dim S As String
Dim N As Long

'FName = Application.GetSaveAsFilename( _
'FileFilter:="XML Files (*.xml),*.xml")
'If FName = False Then
'Exit Sub
'End If
FName = "questions.xml"
Range("A3").Activate
botrow = ActiveCell.End(xlDown).Row
Set RR = Range("A3:I" & botrow) '<<< CHANGE. INCLUDE HEADER ROW.
Set HeaderR = RR(1, 1)
FNum = FreeFile
Open FName For Output Access Write As #FNum
Print #FNum, "<?xml version=""1.0"" encoding=""utf-8""?>"
Print #FNum, "<QUIZ>"
For R = RR(1, 1).Row + 1 To RR.Cells(RR.Cells.Count).Row
N = 0
S = Space(4) & "<QUESTION>" & vbNewLine
For C = RR(1, 1).Column To RR.Cells(RR.Cells.Count).Column
N = N + 1
S = S & Space(8) & "<" & HeaderR(1, N) & ">" & _
CStr(RR.Worksheet.Cells(R, C).Text) & _
"</" & HeaderR(1, N) & ">" & vbNewLine
Next C
```

```
S = S & Space(4) & "</QUESTION>"
Print #FNum, S
Next R
Print #FNum, "</QUIZ>"
Close #FNum
End Sub
```

There is no coverage of the details behind this VBA code or how to utilize it in Excel since that is outside of the scope of this book. If you would like to expand your horizons in VBA programming for Excel, Word, or maybe even Outlook there are many books and sources out in the web for you to utilize. As a matter of fact, the publisher of my book, "Power Outlook" (originally named "Link Em Up on Outlook") is Bill Jelen, better known as Mr Excel. He has published many books on using Excel and VBA.

A - ADDITIONAL RESOURCES

HTML5 Rocks
http://www.html5rocks.com/en/resources

WebReference
http://www.webreference.com/authoring/languages/html/HTML5/index.html

Code Condo
http://codecondo.com/5-tutorials-to-learn-html5-coding/

Beginner HTML5
http://www.elijahmanor.com/beginner-html5-javascript-jquery-backbone-and-css3-resources/

HTML5 Development
http://codecondo.com/11-resources-learn-html5-development-online-beginners/

Tutorials Point
http://www.tutorialspoint.com/html5/index.htm

HTML5 Tutorial
http://www.coreservlets.com/html5-tutorial/

HTML5 Doctor
http://html5doctor.com/resources/

Creative Bloq
HTTP://WWW.CREATIVEBLOQ.COM/WEB-DESIGN/10-TOP-HTML5-RESOURCES-413919

B - SOURCE CODE

You can download a zip file with complete source code for the app designed here and it includes the Excel macro which can be used to create the XML data file used by the app. The download location is

https://wwwords.biz/bookfiles/HTML5Book.zip

You can view and download my other books by starting at

https://wwwords.biz

My company web site should you be interested in business services and other offerings by Link Em Up can be found at https://wwwords.biz

You should note that running the supplied code on your local desktop system can be inconsistent whether using Firefox or Chrome browsers. It has executed properly before on my desktop system from the hard drive using Firefox and it ran well after creating the questions.xml file with the proper type and difficulty settings. The app executes perfectly from a web location, though, across many different platforms. It is also possible to utilize this code coupled with a program such as Phonegap and create a stand-alone app for the iPhone or Android. There is a suggestion which can result in an extremely beneficial learning experience for you as a programmer and also benefit a local organization. Contact a local science museum, wilderness learning center, or maybe even a boy scout troop and suggest that they be the recipient of the output from your experiment. This will give some motivation beyond just trudging through the pages of a book and will give opportunities to customize and improve upon the code presented here.

ABOUT THE AUTHOR

Stephen J. Link is a "computer guy" by profession, an author by hobby, and a Layman in the study of God's Word. He has a computer support book entitled "Link Em Up On Outlook" that was published in 2004 as a paperback (renamed to "Power Outlook" in reprint). He also has over 125 articles covering various topics published on his own blog and independent sites. Various Books have been published covering a number of topics. As a programmer, he has a unique approach to help you master the ability to create the code for automating processes and adding efficiency to your client's or employer's processes.

OTHER WORKS BY STEPHEN LINK AND
LINK EM UP, PUBLISHING DIVISION

Programming and Design

HTML5, CSS3, Javascript and JQuery Mobile Programming: Beginning to End Cross-Platform App Design

Complete, Responsive, Mobile App Design Using Visual Studio: Integrating MySQL Database into your web page

Four Programming Languages Creating a Complete Webscraper Application

Excel Programming through VBA: A Complete Macro Driven Excel 2010 Application

Christian Study

The Journey Along God's Road to Revelation: Complete Scripture Reading in a Year

Volume 1 of the Potter's Clay series: Mold Your Spirit with a Study in Proverbs

Volume 2 of the Potter's Clay series: Mold Your Spirit with a Study in Matthew

Volume 3 of the Potter's Clay series: Mold Your Spirit with a Study in John

Volume 4 of the Potter's Clay series: Mold Your Spirit with another Study in John

Volume 5 of the Potter's Clay series: Mold Your Spirit with a Study in Hebrews

Volume 6 of the Potter's Clay series: Mold Your Spirit with a Study in Acts

Your Computer

Control Your Windows 7 View: Use a Single Wallpaper Across All of Your Screens

Most are in Ebook format and are available across multiple platforms. You can start at https://wwwords.biz to select the book and platform needed. As time allows, these books will be made available for purchase in print.

Social connections

www.facebook.com/stephen.linkemup

www.twitter.com/slinkemup

www.linkedin.com/in/slinkemup